Patrick McCoy

A Girl Called Heather

There was a girl called Heather
who was as light as a feather
the wind blew and blew
up and up she flew
she's now on TV doing the weather!

Cláine Ni hÉalaithe
First Prize: Limerick Competition
Sponsors: Kerry County Council/Kerry County Library

The bald headed man

A bald headed man from Dundee
Lost his wig in a tree
When he looked up and spied it
A hen was inside it
And it laid him an egg for his tea.

Patrick McCoy
Second Prize: Limerick Competition
Sponsors: Kerry County Council/Kerry County Library

Foaming

The bus driver waited for a response. "You're welcome," he said, thinking how tired he was of people looking through him when he spoke. Tired of lugging crowd after crowd from Queens Street to Piccadilly, especially the ungrateful oddballs among them.

Vik's hand shook though he was the only one who noticed as he took the ticket from the driver. He kept his eyes firmly focused on the ground, he wasn't ready for any more yet. The film of cold sweat on his hand soaked into the ticket leaving translucent finger marks on the white strip. Focusing on the empty seats, Vik let his feet guide him through the aisle towards a window seat. He hoped nobody would sit beside him pinning him in, trapping him. That would ruin everything and Vik desperately wanted to succeed at his first attempt.

The seat was relatively comfortable and Vik tried to settle back and relax but his mind raced and his heart pumped the blood loudly through his body. Pieces of foam bulged from holes in the seat where the vinyl had worn. A single thread in some cases was all that held the material together. One false movement and the thread would snap spouting its yellow excrement for the world to see.

As other passengers scouted for seats Vik glanced away, willing them to move on. He wasn't ready to think about them yet. He had to prepare, to settle himself into the situation. Perhaps because of his off-putting glare into space and the tense gait of his body Vik was left alone. They were not ready for him either.

PA 0953 **320588** 8008

Leabharlanna Atha Cliath

00

Items should be returned on or before the last date shown below. Items not already requested by other borrowers may be renewed in person, in writing or by telephone. To renew, please quote the number on the barcode label. To renew online a PIN is required. This can be requested at your local library.
Renew online @ **www.dublincitypubliclibraries.ie**
Fines charged for overdue items will include postage incurred in recovery. Damage to or loss of items will be charged to the borrower.

Leabharlanna Poiblí Chathair Bhaile Átha Cliath
Dublin City Public Libraries

Dublin City
Baile Átha Cliath

Coolock Branch Tel: 8477781

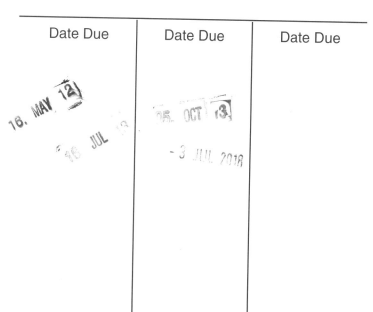

Date Due	Date Due	Date Due
16. MAY 12	05. OCT 13	
06 JUL 13	- 3 JUL 2018	

As the bus pulled away the chatter of the other passengers eventually ceased and after some time Vik took a deep breath and looked back at his fellow passengers. Most had begun to doze, their heads lolling and bobbing as if they were sleep-dancing to some universal rhythm. Though they looked strange and vulnerable Vik envied them. They were at peace. One set of eyes remained open and peered in Vik's direction. Though the woman's gaze was not imposing it startled Vik. He faced forward again, grinding his teeth and pushing his nail into the flesh inside his fist. "What if she knows," he thought. But he realised this was ridiculous. Only a handful knew he had agreed to take this step and only one knew where he would execute it. He closed his eyes and thought of his training.

The woman, taken aback by the young man's reaction to her innocent look, wondered what it was that disturbed him. His olive skin damp, his black hair matted and stuck to his forehead, he rocked backwards and forwards. The other passengers on the bus began to wake up from the fitful sleep the bus allowed, to the realisation that there was something unsettling about the youth who clutched his bag between his fists and emitted a rising stench of panic. A mother put a protective arm around the young child that slept beside her and an old lady began to click through the beads of her rosary.

Vik tried to focus on the holes in the vinyl and to banish all awareness of his fellow passengers. In his training they'd told him that it would feel like everyone was looking at him, but he was sure that what he felt on his skin was real and not the vague concept of paranoia he'd been warned of. The time was fast approaching and the bus driver announced the stop Vik was waiting for. "Stay on until the Piccadilly and then carry out the Task", they had said. Vik chanted this to himself. This simple direction was all he could think of and almost more than he could bear. Before he knew what he was doing his hand left the bag he hugged and tore at the single piece of string holding the foam inside the vinyl. The hole grew before his eyes and the open wound exposed the entrails of the seat to the air. Vik turned to see if anyone had noticed. "They know," he thought. The bus pulled into his stop.

The driver watched the awkward, dark youth make his way towards the top of the bus and search through his bag manically. He grew nervous and reached for the panic button concealed under the steering wheel. Young blokes were capable of anything these days.

Vik found what he was searching for and pulled the piece of paper from his bag. He looked at it and made a quick mark with a pen, before staring directly into the eyes of the driver. The noise of the bus and of the street outside faded and Vik pushed all distraction away. He counted silently to ten as his training had taught him. He had come so far alone. Summoning all his courage and never losing eye contact Vik began to speak "Th . . . "

The bus driver moved back from the panic button. His expression softened. In Vik's hand the direction sheet shook violently. *"Task 4: Travel alone on bus no. 10 to stop 6"*, an illegible tick had been scrawled in the box.

"Make eye contact with the driver".

"Th . . . ", the seconds passed agonisingly. Vik took a final breath and his mind briefly cleared.

"Thank you" he said.

Ruth O'Sullivan
Winner: Writers' Week Originals – Short Story
Sponsors: Bank of Ireland

Sitting Still

Shadows cast by moons will blaze with light,
And sunlight's shine will darken all therein,
The stars will burn to bronze upon your sight,
And Gaia, too, will tremble through her skin.
Those born blind will cry with what they see,
The deaf and dumb will sing with what they hear,
The lame will dance to cure their malady,
The scared will laugh to frighten off their fear.
Within, your dark will flare to roaring flame,
The rage has waited long; you'll see it ravage,
Wildness does not bow and turn to tame,
But sits still until its master's ripe to savage.
When you break free, the world will break free too,
Sitting still, this is my plea to you.

Sean Godley
Winner: Writers' Week Originals – Short Poem
Sponsors: Bank of Ireland

Athenian Goddesses

*F*riday lunchtime and why is there never enough time? I try to avert my eyes as I sidle past the rows of enticing glossiness. But somehow I can never resist a fleeting glimpse of Utopia. Athenian goddesses smile mockingly at me. Look at me, I am not having a bad hair day or my stomach isn't gurgling from a night of over indulgence. Here I am posing on a sun kissed beach with no visible sign of mother hood apparent when I display my bikini clad concave stomach.

Guilt consumes me when I read about how her children just merely lodged themselves in her lithe body without causing her the merest inconvenience. They popped out and spluttered their first breath while she was already conniving to slip back into her size eight jeans. What a glorious existence they must have, being placed on this earth to merely torment us poor less fortunate mortals.

The clouds of self denial are evaporating around me. The time has come to relinquish the pretence. My tumble drier isn't realy the culprit to be blamed for my ever shrinking clothes. Another style queen is pouting at me her skinny hips adorned with a skin tight pair of hipsters. She is not a teeny bopper so my theory that "the more mature mom," is bound to have more sizeable hips and a few wear and tear bumps doesn't quite hold up.

The family gatherings are the worst. The last time I saw Auntie Maeve I was childless and damage limitation was not a word in my vocabulary. Now even with my black body skimming garments I still can't hide the signs that her beady eyes are scanning me for. "You have put on a bit of weight have you?" The triumphant glee exudes from her voice. Brought down to earth now am I not? A gnawing reminder that I am not going to escape my genetic inheritance no matter how opposed I am to it. Why couldn't she have said "congratulations on your promotion, well done for buying the new car or your house is a credit to you?"

She has thrown the truth at me and now it has an external voice. The inner insecurity now has sustenance. There is no joy left now, the aroma of the freshly baked sausage rolls or the crispy coating on the southern fried chicken or even the sparkling bottle of white all suddenly devoid of pleasure to me. All I am conscious of are the rolls of fat on my inner thighs wrestling with each other as I haul my bulk towards the door.

Driving my car is a tortuous experience. It is a tranquil evening with the scarlet sun still peeping out from beneath the crimson clouds. No good. My spare tire protrudes limply over the strained belt on my trousers. Loose unfettered skin the true evidence of my over indulgence.

Home to face my wardrobe. I sort through the dwindling few items that haven't been stuffed in the drawer or moved guiltily to a less conspicuous place so their wanton redundancy won't torment me. In desperation I reach for my consolation jeans, spacious and comfortable they will redeem me.

Deep inwards breaths, sweat glowing on my forehead but they are on. I face my enemy, a brass full length mirror. Where am I? There is some imposter staring back at me. Her round pale face, her eyes encased with purple tinted lines, her double chin hiding her once slender neck. Heaving misshapen mounds are struggling within a too small bra. This unfortunate woman has no waist only unfathomable mounds of sagging white flesh, with embroidered veins protruding forth.

The back view is worse. Two misshapen cushions with the foam peeping through causing large eneven crinkling on the skin reaching all the way down to the knees. Where have I gone, why can't I be allowed to see myself the way that I still feel?

What is today's mother supposed to do? There are four persons to be gotten up every day, dinners are eaten on the run, a boss who makes me sell my soul when I enter the premises and pretend that I don't have a life outside his four walls.

My home is beautiful if somewhat empty, my children have every-thing except my time, my husband shares the bills another unwilling participant in our infinite quest, where is the time to be an Athenian Goddess in Celtic Tiger Ireland?

Mary Kelly Godley
Winner: Writers' Week Originals – Humorous Essay
Sponsors: Bank of Ireland

The Bog Menagerie

"That there's Turlough," says Bob. Bob is the supervisor. He is in a Harris Tweed sports coat and matching trousers, red tie and turned-down wellingtons. Everybody's in turned-down wellingtons. Bob's pointing through the steam of the bleach house with a hand in a rubber glove. Standing beside a big pale-green machine about twelve puddles away is a short man with jet black straight hair and slightly yellow skin. If I didn't know better I'd think there was a bit of the exotic Oriental about him. Turlough's in navy overalls, and when he moves away across the floor he has a definite waddly walk. For some reason he hasn't turned down the tops of his wellingtons. He stands out a mile.

The whole place is awash with water and chemicals. Moisture content is high.

"And Turlough drives the bleacher," says Bob. We go towards the machine Turlough has just left. "See, the cloth comes out of the bleacher here." We watch the cloth come off a roller and fold itself up into a big box on wheels. "Someday," says Bob, "when we know you're a man to be trusted, maybe you'll get to drive the bleacher." He throws a wink at me.

Then he takes me to the store and gives me my wellingtons. I put them on and turn down the tops.

"You'll fit in," said Bob. "It's not everybody does," he says.

"Sure," I say. Bob is already walking away.

The place is full of Protestants, and a few Fenians keeping quiet. Turlough is one of the Fenians. I suspect I've been put to work with him because nobody else will.

But I'm quiet myself, and I get on all right with Turlough.

"You'll get the hang of it," says Turlough, and then doesn't speak the rest of the day. I've seen his hands by then. He's got webbed fingers, the skin coming up to the middle knuckles. For the first hour or so I watch him pick up shears with them, and press buttons, and pour chemicals, but then I just forget about them.

One day he says, "It's a very old Irish name, you know, Turlough. Kings of Ireland were called Turlough. Earls off on their flight. All that kind of thing."

"Sure," I say. I always agree with him. Another week passes. Turlough's been thinking up some more things to say.

"Are you interested in the olden days? The stories and the kings and queens and all?" He's not looking at me as he asks this, because knowing about the history of Ireland is all Fenian stuff, like speaking Gaelic and Irish dancing and calies or however you spell them.

"Sure," I say, so he tells me about a cattle raid, and kings setting each other challenges, and a queen grabbing land. This is in between wheeling big boxes of cloth around and treading it up through the bleacher and putting plastic jugs of chemicals into steel troughs.

On every shift now I'm offered a story about some aspect of Ireland's past, and every time I say, "sure". Sometimes they're stories about the little people and banshees and giants.

And then Turlough asks me what I'm doing on Sunday afternoon, which surprises me.

"Sitting in my room reading," I say, which is the truth. So then he asks me if I'd like to go to his house. I'm not just surprised. I'm astonished. He says he's got some books I'd enjoy looking at, and a few old bits and pieces. He calls them "artefacts". He tells me he lives down at the Lough shore, and I could cycle there. I'm more astonished again. He means the lough shore of Lough Neagh, and it's only Fenians who live down round the Lough shore.

"Sure," I say.

So on Sunday I'm on the bike and peddling along holding a bit of paper in one hand and trying to follow Turlough's instructions about how to get there. It's July by then and the weather's at it's best I turn off a small road lined with hawthorn onto a smaller lane covered in fuchsias and briers, and then off that lane onto this track heading off among the bogs and whins and the odd sticking-up rowan. There's a solitary roof in the distance and that's the only sign of humanity. There's nothing behind the house but the waters of the Lough.

I get off the bike in a farmyard. There's hens scrabbling about, and a nanny goat tied with a rope to the bottom of a bush, and a big fat hoker of a pig in a pen at the side of the house. I wonder if Turlough slaughters the animals himself. I suspect he does. A fishing rod stands against the wall, and a net hangs over the roof of a shed. There's no dogs, which surprises me. I'm thinking about getting back on the bike when Turlough comes out of the front door. He's wearing tan overalls instead of the navy. He's still got the wellingtons on.

"Agh god hello there," he says. We go inside and he shows me a couple of books in Gaelic, which I can't make head nor tail of. There's a shelf of Irish history books in English, which seem interesting. There's geometric shapes made out of dried and woven Lough reeds hanging on the walls. He explains the significance of these to me. He shows me a glass case in a corner, with figures of people and animals carved out of a heavy black wood in it. "Bog-oak" Turlough calls the wood. Some of the carvings are of ordinary people and farm animals, and some are of things somebody must have imagined. Turlough makes tea, which is served out in wee delicate cups. There's butter and fruity soda bread, homemade-looking. I examine his hands, but they are pale and very clean as always, so I eat the bread. The wee webs between the fingers I hardly notice now.

It seems very comfortable here. The small farm, the books, the sense of a past.

He takes me out to the shed where the net is, and unlocks the door and shows me an old turf spade, and a butter churner. "Before sixteen hundred," he says. The wood feels more like stone. "Petrified in the Lough water," explains Turlough. I'm not as comfortable in the shed. Then he shows me some bottles, bits of metal harness, a spoon, part of a sword. I'm thinking about the lock on the door. He tells me he's found all these things in the bog while digging turf.

"I'd like to be out in the air again," I tell Turlough. "Bad chest, you know," I say.

We take a walk up a track to the Lough shore and he shows me where he fishes, and talks of the pollen, which is a freshwater herring. He tells me that Finn McCool the giant pulled up a big sod which left the hole that made the Lough, which is a story I know already, and he tells me of "waterguns," and of the horse-god Eochu, which I don't know anything about.

"Do you like swimming?" he says.

"I love swimming," I say. "I'd be in the water all day in the summer I could." I haven't swam for years. I'm wondering how long I'm going to be here.

Then he says the dinner's near ready, if I don't mind eating late. I can't understand how he's cooked the dinner while standing looking at the water with me. But we go back into the house. The plates with the soda bread and butter have gone, and there's blue willow pattern dinner plates on the table. Turlough takes a pot of spuds off the range and there's fish in a dish and cabbage in a sauce pan. Turlough tells me the fish is pollen. He serves out the pollen and spuds and cabbage and we sit at the table again and eat. I'm wondering what the lavatory arrangements are like when I hear a rattle upstairs, and then a small thump. There's somebody up there walking about I say nothing.

"We're plagued with the mice here," says Turlough. He's seen me looking up.

"Sure," I say. "I think it's time to go, Turlough," I say.

"I've been thinking about things," says Turlough. "Thinking things over."

"You're good at that, Turlough," I say. It's the truth.

"I've been thinking that I've asked my own sort over here and none of them ever came. Then you came."

"There's nothing to it, Turlough," I say. "Time was hanging heavy on my hands and all that."

"But you know what I mean," he says. "Coming down, spending time talking, eating food. Down here at the Lough shore and all." I do know what he means. "So I'd like you to meet somebody," he says.

"Sure," I say. "Would that be the one upstairs?"

"I'll tell you," he says. "It's the sister. She's been in the bath. She loves the bath. She'll be down in a minute."

After a while there's a light padding sounds on the stairs. A woman younger than Turlough comes in. She's wearing a short green dress. There's funny lighting in this house, for her skin looks a bit green like the dress. She's got lovely long black hair still wet from the bath. When I think about it her skin seems wet as well. She's got completely webbed fingers. She's barefooted. She sees me looking.

"Yes. The feet as well," she says. Her voice is wonderful, in a slightly rasping, croaking sort of way.

"This is Aine," say Turlough.

I just sit looking at her. I've never seen a woman so lovely, nor so odd.

"Well, I did what I said," says Turlough. He's speaking to his sister. "This is Jim," he says. "Your gentleman caller."

Aine comes and sits down at the table.

"Are you enjoying your dinner?" she asks.

"Sure," I say. "I've never had this fish before."

"We eat them all the time. I catch them myself," says Aine. "After you've let your dinner go down in you would you like a swim? Let's go along the Lough share for walk until then."

"Sure," I say. Up close her skin is very smooth, her eyes dark green and wide, her mouth all pouty lipped. I feel a strong desire to kiss her.

"I'll do the dishes," says Turlough.

As we walk she talks about the trees and the grasses and the insects. She's very good on all of this and especially the insects. Outside the house that impression of her skin being green is confirmed. I realise she still isn't wearing any shoes. She talks about the weather conditions and gives a forecast for the next five days. "Very heavy rain on Tuesday," she says. She seems pleased. When we come to a stile she hops over it in one go. I climb after her. I have certainly never known a woman like Aine before.

"Time to swim!" she cries. She runs ahead towards the water, and when I catch up with her she's already pulling the short dress off over her head. She's naked underneath. Her whole body is very firm, with dark speckled marks on her back, otherwise she's pale green and slightly shining. The next thing she leaps from the mud of the bank far out into the water. I undress and wade in after her in my underwear. I'm gasping and shivering. She's nowhere to be seen. Then her head pops up far away. All I can see is the eyes and the top of her head. Then she's gone again. Next thing she's popping up beside me, and pulling me under with her. She rubs her skin up against mine, and it's all very exciting.

Encouraged, I swim far out also, ducking and diving, grasping her legs underwater, sinking to the bottom, bobbing up again. How strongly muscled those thighs are.

"This is wonderful," she says in her slightly croaky voice. "It's much better than being alone." She pulls my underwear off. She's flushed in a sort of green way, and laughing. When we eventually come ashore she pulls me over on top of her and kisses me and licks me and we make wonderful slippery love.

We wash off the mud and dress and make our way back to the house. It has all been very exciting, but also very strange and unsettling. As we have a last kiss behind a fuchsia bush at the end of the track, Aine says,

"I'm going upstairs for another bath. Turlough will want a word with you."

As I get on my bicycle Turlough says,

"Aine and I would both like you to come back again."

I think about all the green skin and the dark speckles on the back, how she leapt the stile and into the water, and all the webbing on the hands and feet. I also remember how excited I got. I don't know if I can take all this again.

"I'm not sure," I say. "I don't know if . . . if . . ."

"She sleeps a lot in the winter," says Turlough. "Come back. She'll miss you. She's already very fond of you. I can tell."

I'm trying to say "sure", but I can't. I shake my head.

"She needs somebody," goes on Turlough. "She's intelligent and well read and great company. She's a good person."

"I'm sure she is," I say. Then I have a thought. "I'm engaged to a woman now in England," I say. "She's been there for months, working all hours god sends, making the money for us to get married on."

"Ccccagggh," says Turlough. Its nearly a croak.

"Her name is Myrtle," I go on. "After the bush." Turlough is nodding.

"I'll tell Aine," he says. And he is gone.

On Monday I'm working again with Turlough. I talk about the weather while measuring out bleach, but he says very little about anything and nothing about the weekend. On Tuesday there is very heavy rain. On Wednesday I hang around Turlough after putting acetic acid in the steel trough but there are no stories of Ireland's past. On Thursday Bob the charge hand's Harris Tweed suit appears through the steam. Production is down, he says. Is everything's all right with Turlough and me? It's the first time he's come near the bleacher since I started.

"Sure," I say. Bob is already turning away.

The rest of the day I hover around Turlough while he sews webs of cloth together but there is only silence. On Friday I ask him about Aine.

"She's very sad," says Turlough. "She sits in the bath all day. There's no food on the table. I've caught her crying more times."

I've never been missed like that before. I remember her green skin, her webbed hands and feet, her sleek constantly wet-looking hair. I think about her green skin again. Her firm back and the dark speckled marks.

"She isn't even carving the wee bog-oak figures any more," says Turlough.

I feel sad for poor Aine. I've got scraps of linen around my feet inside my wellingtons trying to keep them dry, and I re-arrange them while thinking. I remember her very well-muscled legs wrapped around me.

"I'll come down on Sunday," I tell Turlough.

"It's going to be wet on Sunday," says Turlough. "Good for catching the pollen," he says.

"There's no Myrtle," I say. I look at him through the clouds of steam. He seems to be smiling.

I can see Aine catching the pollen now. She wouldn't be using the rod or the net. In her teeth maybe. Ducking and diving, catching them under water, the webbed hands and feet so efficient, wrestling them, throwing them flapping onto the Lough shore. Her green skin shining, dripping. I see the puddles on the bleach house floor, the steel troughs, the endless water running off the pipes overhead. Most of all I see Bob's red tie appearing and disappearing through the steam as he and the rest of the work force meet and talk together amongst themselves and keep away from Turlough and me.

"Sure," I say. "Sure."

Ferran Anderson
Winner: The Bryan MacMahon Short Story Award
Sponsors: The Ireland Funds

YOU MUST KNOW EVERYTHING
A collection of poems

Hospice

In this airy bright cool room
– its windows open to the Spring,
two beds, one bare, unoccupied,
one left an hour ago – she reads.

Of the Browning's life in Italy,
the odd, dead, love between them;
their little spaniel dog; their rooms,
still visited by a few it seems.

(For the distanced thrilling
of those two, the views of Venice,
passionate deceit,
imagined voices . . .)

She smokes a cigarette,
then, dressed in a white gown,
not hers, walks down the short
sun-blooming corridors

to the cold, burning needle
placed to her breast –
in another white, tall room,
with an almost identical view of Spring.

What time is it?

On the pear tree at six
the blackbird speaks.

He talks of no creation
that we, translated to his garden

and looking back, could ever see. I go inside.
The back door has the same, jarring slide.

Again, against the quiet, I rage.
You sit, forever reading the same page

at the table just behind me.
You listen once more, patiently,

to my ideas of Time. The world ever Present;
Past and Future irredeemably absent;

this room a delusion – what is out of sight
simply chaos, juggling light . . .

'Yes, love. But . . .' I sit. In a moment I'll turn,
and the past turn

with me, and you will not be there
nor will be, smiling into the darkening air.

The English Lovers

Make a cage.
The gate shakes.
Warm my hand.
The hat falls.

He sees me.
He feels wet.
We went to bed.
He fed the bees.

Fire shines
Vines give wine.
Kites rise to the sky.
Lips are red.

Fir swims.
Birds sing.
Grirls spin.
He rides.

He holds the rose to my nose.
The dove took food.

I can tame his bird.
I am not old.
My bird hops on my hand.

The red sun sets.
The moon is white.
This stone feels hard.
Ice makes the hand cold.

It is not safe to play with fire.
There is no harm in the dark.
It is a sin to wish for it.

(A poem made by using unaltered phrases from
Curso de Inglés, by Professor H. MacVeigh,
published in Madrid in 1888)

William Palmer

The Exhumation of Lizzie Siddal

A fire is lit beside the grave:
Officers of the Court, the diggers,
the poet's representative, all look in . . .
The body is raised – and, miracle,

she is quite unchanged. The book wrapped
in her lovely hair is mildewed – and the friend
leans down, weeping, and lifts the book
and, with it, some hair parts from the head.

Oh perfect. Perfect. Trembling, he holds the book.
The coffin lid's replaced; the guide ropes
are let down again, lowering the resealed box
into that damp, rectangular, glistening place.

He clutches the book, the book –
a small, square shape containing words;
the flames, dwindling, gather to one last blaze
and shine and smoulder in her red-gold hair.

William Palmer
Winner: Poetry Collection
Sponsors: The Ireland Funds

I was Sitting

I was sitting
watching,
a man's job, tough,
but someone's gotta do it, when he squeaks,
bit muffled like,
"Take over Mum I've had enough"
and just his head and eyes were out,
the beautifullest eyes I ever sees
and I says "Son, you're a caution and no mistake"
and he winked at me and I thought
there's something odd
such happy large clear shining eyes
but upside down when he said
"Hi. You must be my Dad"
it was coming right out the back of his head
and I said "It's a wise kid,
my son, that knows his father"
and his nose was where his ear
should be, but each bit,
by God, so individually pretty
then he plops full out,
a mite streaky
with the blood and gunge,

his shoulders creeping edge –
ways out of his bum,
his knees all backward like a nag,
his feet turned round, his groin a tangle,
no cobblers, only shreds of Hampton,
"Jeez" he says "quick put me to the breast,
it's just 11, they're open!"

"Son" I says "Meet your Mum"
and sotto voky to the Philippina,
"Auntie, just settle him on her chest,
leave them scissors for a moment,
let the cord alone".
"Go on my son, back in a jiff"
and I sidles off with
the Obst. and Gny. bloke who would've
been the proverbial white as a, if
he hadn't been dusky as a power cut
and I says ". . . quiet now, Tiger, if he can hear and
understand and speak we must be gentle and keeping out of
earshot . . . "

"You babby got no suck response and obstruction in da throat,
we put an intravenous on, couple of tubes via trach. OK?
pass him aesophyglottis, an den we emergency de bowel an waterworks".

"Hold it, Panther.
No. You put 'em
in a private room
and cover up the mirror.

His outsides is all back
to front and higgledy pig, it's a pony
to a monkey
his insides ain't gonna be back
to back and hunky dory.
He won't be thanking you for a lifetimes hospital
under your scalpel.
No suck response. Not viable.
He's pupped here clutching his pass out chit
in his beautiful tiny twisted fist.
You're a wise old
Leopard.
Gazelles eh?
Survival of
the fittest."

So, just
the three of us ("Keep his Mum knocked out" I told 'em,
"would you mind") and he lay in her arms.
I said "Son, you're the best and prettiest son a Dad could wish"
and he said "Why're you crying Dad?" "Happiness"
I said "Son, just sheer happiness."

Keith Francis
Winner: Single Poem Competition
Sponsors: The Ireland Funds

Grace and Truth

*W*e seemed to be winning the war at last.

The Allies had landed in Normandy and were fighting their way across the North of Europe. Jokes crept back into people's conversations and their faces became less grey and stressed-looking.

I was in my first parish in West Wicklow, forty families scattered across the hills and low valleys, not badly off; the land was good, their cattle fed well and they were regular church attenders; they came on their bicycles and in their pony traps and brought us butter and fine brown eggs and the odd bottle of poitín.

One summer day she came to me in my study. She crossed the room and sat in the chair opposite my desk. She folded her hands neatly on her knee.

"I think," she said, "that it is time we had a child."

I put down my pen and looked at her. "Why?"

"I think it is expected of us. My parents are . . . my parents are getting on, you know, and I think . . . "

Her face was red. She stared past me out through the window at the garden.

"You know what this entails, don't you?"

She nodded.

There was a long silence.

"I think you are probably right," I said at last.

"Thank you." It was a whisper.

She stood up and came round the desk and stood beside me. She laid a hand on my shoulder and bent and kissed the top of my head.

"Thank you." She whispered the word again and left the room.

I got up and stood by the window staring out at the bright garden and I longed to be wrapped in the loving arms of God, any God, just someone stronger than I was, someone who loved me without reserve, someone wise and gentle and all-seeing, someone who I knew did not exist.

Jennifer Johnston
Shortlisted for Kerry Group Irish Fiction Award
Reprinted with kind permission of Headline and Review

The Sea

Chloe put a pellet of bread into her mouth and wetted it with spit and took it out again and kneaded it in her fingers with slow deliberation and took leisurely aim and threw it at me, but the wad fell short. "Chloe!" her mother said, a wan reproach, and Chloe ignored her and smiled at me her cat's thin, gloating smile. She was a cruel-hearted girl, my Chloe. For her amusement of a day I would catch a handful of grasshoppers and tear off one of their back legs to prevent them escaping and put the twitching torsos in the lid of a polish tin and douse them in paraffin and set them alight. How intently, squatting with hands pressed on her knees, she would watch the unfortunate creatures as they seethed, boiling in their own fat.

She was making another spit-ball. "Chloe, you are disgusting," Mrs Grace said with a sigh, and Chloe, all at once bored, spat out the bread and brushed the crumbs from her lap and rose and walked off sulkily into the shadow of the pine tree.

Did Connie Grace catch my eye! Was that a complicit smile? With a heaving sigh she turned and lay down supine on the bank with her head leaning back on the grass and flexed one leg, so that suddenly I was allowed to see under her skirt along the inner side of her thigh all the way up to the hollow of her lap and the plump mound there sheathed in tensed white cotton. At once everything began to slow. Her emptied glass fell over in a swoon and a last drop of wine ran to the rim and hung an instant glittering and then fell. I stared and stared, my brow growing hot and my palms wet. Mr Grace under his hat seemed to be smirking at me but I did not care, he could smirk al he liked. His big wife, growing bigger by the moment, a foreshortened, headless giantess at whose huge feet I crouched in what felt almost like fear, gave a sort of wriggle and raised her knee higher still, revealing the crescent-shaped crease at the full-fleshed back of her leg where her rump began. A drumbeat in my temples was making the daylight dim. I was aware of the throbbing sting in my gouged ankle. And now from far off in the ferns there came a thin, shrill sound, an archaic pipe-note piercing through the lacquered air, and Chloe, up at the tree, scowled as if called to duty and bent and plucked a blade of grass and pressing it between her thumbs blew an answering note out of the conch-shell of her cupped hands.

John Banville
Shortlisted for the Kerry Group Irish Fiction Award
Reprinted with kind permission of Pan MacMillan Publishers Ltd

A Long Long Way

The whisper went round among the companies, and even if not everyone knew the name, soft words were said, and heads were dipped, in the proper funereal manner. But many knew the name, and many knew the story of the man in his fifties who had insisted on going up the line and into danger, a person with a thousand advantages, the brother, as Willie had put it, of "your man", the leader of the Irish Party at Westminster, whom Willie's own father had deemed a scoundrel. But it didn't seem so to Willie. The whisper went round and when it was said to Father Buckley, the priest openly wept. In fact, he burst into tears right in front of the corporal who said it to him. Then it became like a common death, like a person close to them all had died. For Willie Redmond was dead. He died in an old style, twice wounded, roaring at the disappearing backs of his men to keep going and watch out in the attack. Stretcher bearers attached to the 36th Division took him to their regimental aid post. Ulster accents eased him into death, minds that maybe before the war would have looked on such a person with traditional horror.

Willie Dunne bumped into Father Buckley in the shit-house. Of course, a shit-house had no roof, so could you call it a house, but there it was. The priest had his usual penance of mild dysentery, so Willie Dunne had to wait while the man strained over the hole in the ground, and shot out streams of thin yellow shit. At last relief seemed to return to the anguished features.

"I'm sorry for your trouble, Father," said Willie.

"I'll offer it up, Willie. Not much choice."

"Well, I meant, you know, that poor man dying, Father. The MP."

Father Buckley looked at him. His face broke into a smile.

"We were talking about him only the other day, weren't we, Willie?"

"Yes, sir."

"Everyone says he was a fine man. And he was. I had dinner with him one time, Willie. He was full of fun and stories. A most sincere and gentle man. You know I walked into Whytschaete myself to see what I could see. And there they were, back-slapping each other, North and South, and it was a grand moment. It was Willie Redmond's moment, if only he could have seen it. But he was killed. He was killed. That is the pity of it."

"Of course, Father."

"We have to keep our chins up, as the English fellas say. It's hard sometimes. But we've got to try. It'll all turn out right in the end. It's God's will."

"I hope so, Father."

"I hope so too, Willie."

But the talk didn't seem to be over.

"Are you all right, Father?" said Willie.

"I will be all right – when this bloody war is over."

"Of course," said Willie.

"Yes," said the priest.

Sebastian Barry
Shortlisted for Kerry Group Irish Fiction Award
Reprinted with kind permission of Faber & Faber Ltd

Utterly Monkey

He met Wee Jim and Del from his scout troup at the Oldtown Corner. They were waiting for Jacksy, the same boy who would later shoot a bullet through each of Geordie's calves. Del opened his rucksack and showed Danny seven or eight cans of Top Deck shandy and three Hamlet cigars. He hushed his voice, as if the contraband was asleep: *We're going to get wrecked.* Just then Jacksy came slouching around the corner, hunched with his hands tucked tight in his jeans. *Awright lads.* His voice was lower than everyone else's. He was a skinny cock-sure kid who suffered from eczema. His hands reminded Danny of sunburn. He rarely took them out of his pockets.

They took a can each. Danny wasn't sure if the Top Deck was alcoholic. It didn't seem to say on the cans although it tasted like beer, but less sour. They decided to head over to the wide kerb outside Martin's Chemists.

There was a bench there and, after five minutes of standing around her, the old biddy on it got up and tottered off, clutching her shopping with both arms in front of her, as if the boys had been very taken with her cat food and her toilet roll.

The way things worked was this. After school, the boys would walk home together, anything from four or five to ten of them. Some days they'd "shoot some pool" down Eastwood's Pool Hall, other days buy brown paper bags of vinegary chips from the Brewery Grill and eat them in the back attic room of McGurk's Undertakers, whose youngest son, Wee Jim, was part of the gang. James McGurk was not only an undertaker, but also, like Danny's dad, an estate agent. Danny had often wondered if business for the latter was dependent on the former. He must benefit by being around when the relatives discussed the sale of the deceased's caravan or bungalow or castle. In the back attic, reached by walking through two offices and along a curtain-corridor that ran along the side of the funeral parlour, Big Jim McGurk had stored or dumped about fifteen mattresses and a threadbare snooker table short several balls, mostly reds. There were also, propped along the wall, three display coffins. It lent the place the look of a particularly louche Pharaoh's tomb. It was an odd place for an after-school club. One of them, Del maybe, had done a sign with a black marker – *The Coffin Boys* – and Blu-tacked it to the wall beside the big oak boxes. The top left-hand corner had come away and leaned outward like the gelled tufts most of them sported.

Nick Laird
Shortlisted for the Kerry Group Irish Fiction Award
Reprinted with kind permission of HarperCollins Publishers

The Family on Paradise Pier

*I*t was not the fact that Art had left for Russia which hurt her, but that he never said goodbye to any of them. Even a noviciate entering a monastery rarely denied himself a last farewell to those he loved. Because Eva knew that Art loved his family although he had never returned to Donegal after her wedding. Mother only learnt that he was in Moscow when Mr Ffrench received a letter last week from a friend there who had met him.

Freddie gently prised Mother's letter from Eva's hand and read the news for himself whilst his heavily pregnant wife gazed out of the drawing room window of Glanmire House to where Mikey, Freddie's man, stood by the car, patiently waiting to accompany his master to the station. Eva knew that Freddie would wet his lips in the select lounge of the Imperial Hotel in Castlebar before boarding the Dublin train.

"It's for the best for all of you," Freddie announced. "At least now he won't be able to disgrace you, or if he does he'll be so far away that it will not be in front of anyone who counts. And, you know, with Art gone, the young chap may buck up. It's not too late for Brendan to get into some decent college. Oxford will hardly take him now, but only a fool judges a man by the colour of his school tie."

Eva had often heard her husband repeat this line, carefully watching the company for any perceived slight about how he had lacked the money to attend a top public school.

Freddie was relieved by this news about Art, though they had only met briefly at the wedding, an awkward encounter between two men whom Eva loved. It now felt like years since Thomas had played the bagpipes in his kilt as Eva's wedding party wound through Dunkineely. Locals had cheered as barefoot children raced after the Wolseley that bore her away to Mayo, with bonfires marking her arrival in Turlough where the Fitzgeralds had reigned for centuries. Her books were still stored in a trunk with her canvasses and easel. They were things she seemed unable to unpack, being too busy trying to appear like a young Protestant wife of social standing. She fretted over invitations to tennis parties and dinners at Turlough Park held by Freddie's uncle on one of his trips back home. He found it cheaper to maintain his family in a rented French villa rather than upkeep his Irish mansion. An avenging mob had ransacked the original house after "Mad" George Robert Fitzgerald's public hanging in 1786, leading to the hasty erection of Glanmire House as a stopgap family home until the grandiose splendour of a new house at Turlough Park was completed. Glanmire House was as large as the Manor House in Dunkineely, but it was impossible to live so close to Turlough Park without feeling in every way the poor relation.

Freddie handed her back the letter, too much of a gentleman to read beyond Mother's news about Art. "Let's see if he lasts longer in Moscow than the other lunatic."

"Mr Ffrench is nice," Eva protested.

Freddie laughed, downing the dregs of whiskey in his glass.

Dermot Bolger
Shortlisted for the Kerry Group Irish Fiction Award
Reprinted with kind permission of HarperCollins Publishers

Tearmann

RADHARC 1

Tráthnóna.

AINGEAL ina suí os comhair an bhoird, ZOË toabh thiar den bhord, á ceistiú, foirmeacha ar an mbord roimpi. GRETA ina seasamh taobh le ZOË, tóirse ina láimh aici, á lonrú ar aghaidh AINGEAL.

ZOË   Ainm? Ainm, a deir mé?

Ligeann GRETA osna. Caitheann ZOË drochshúil uirthi agus leanann uirthi ag ceistiú AINGEAL.

ZOË   Ainm?
              (ag scríobh) Aingeal. Go bhfios dúinn.
              Gnéas – bean, is cosúil.
              Aois – aois?
              Thart ar thríocha, déarfainn.
              Stádas – neamhphósta.
              Páistí? Gan páistí – go bhfios dúinn.
              Gairm – gairm?
              Caithfidh tú na ceisteanna a fhreagairt.
              Gairm?
              Ní thuigimse an fáth a mbíonn tú mar seo.
              An dtuigeann tusa?

AINGEAL   Ní thuigim.

ZOË   Tosóidh mé arís: ainm? Céard is ainm duit?

AINGEAL   Aingeal is ainm dom.

ZOË   Is maith is eol dúinn gurb é Aingeal d'ainm. Céard é d'ainm
              ceart?

AINGEAL   Aingeal.

Celia de Fréine

ZOË	Is maith is eol duitse nach é sin d'ainm ceart – nach bhfuil ann ach leasainm.
AINGEAL	Níl a fhios agam an é m'ainm ceart é nó nách é.
ZOË	Abairt! Tá sí tar éis abairt a chur le chéile, cé gurb abairt dhiúltach í. Ráiteas diúltach. Tosóidh mé arís. Don uair dheireanach. Céard is ainm duit?
AINGEAL	Aingeal.
ZOË	*(go mífhoighneach)* Céard as duit?
AINGEAL	Tír i bhfad i gcéin.
ZOË	A hainm?
AINGEAL	Trasna na dtonnta. I bhfad i gcéin.
ZOË	Cén saghas rialtais atá inti?
AINGEAL	Deachtóireacht.
ZOË	Ainm an deachtóra?
AINGEAL	An Fear Mór.
ZOË	Agus a rialtas?
AINGEAL	Deachtóir atá ann.
ZOË	An fáth ar tháinig tú anseo?
AINGEAL	D'éalaigh mé.
ZOË	Cén fáth ar éalaigh tú?
AINGEAL	Tháinig mé anseo.
ZOË	Cén fáth?
AINGEAL	Deachtóir is ea é.
ZOË	Céard a rinne sé ort?

AINGEAL   An Fear Mór.

GRETA   Is leor an méid sin, ZOË.

De réir a chéile soiléirítear gur ceistiúchán bréagach atá ar siúl ag an triúr.

ZOË   Tá freagraí uaim, Greta.

GRETA   Nach bhfuil do dhóthain agat anois?

ZOË   Bhí mé ar tí briseadh tríd. Bhí eolas úrnua faighte agam: deachtóir, tír i bhfad i gcéin.

GRETA   Nach leor é sin?

ZOË   Dá mba leor, ní bhéinn ag iarraidh leanúint ar aghaidh.

GRETA   Sílim gur éirigh go geal linn inniu.
Go raibh maith agat, Aingeal.

Múchann GRETA an tóirse. Seasann ZOË agus AINGEAL. Cuirtear an bord i leataobh. Tosaíonn ZOË ag scuabadh an úrláir.

AINGEAL   An raibh mé go maith, GRETA? Ar oir na freagraí daoibh?

GRETA   D'oir, a stór.

ZOË   Ní raibh said pioc sásúil.

GRETA   Tá tú ró-dhian uirthi, ZOË.
D'éirigh go geal leat inniu, Aingeal

AINGEAL   Go raibh maith agat, GRETA. Is tuisceanach an bhean thú.

ZOË   Tá mé spréachta ag an mbeirt agaibh. Caithfidh sí dóthain freagraí – na freagraí cearta – a bheith aici má tá sí ag iarraidh fanacht sa tír seo. B'in an fáth a raibh mé á ceistiú. Ach ní chuidíonn sí liom ariamh. Agus tusa á gríosadh – tá tú níos measa ná í!

GRETA   Thug sí a hainm duit. Agus sonraí leis.

AINGEAL	Thug, nár thug? Go raibh maith agat, GRETA. Tá mé ag dul i bhfeabhas, nach bhfuil? Abair liom go bhfuil mé ag dul i bhfeabhas.
GRETA	Tá, a stór. Tá.
AINGEAL	Seans go gcreidfidh said mé?
GRETA	Seans mór millteach.
AINGEAL	Go raibh maith agat, GRETA. Cuireann tú mo mháthair i gcuimhne dom.
GRETA	Do mháthair? An cuimhin leat do mháthair?
AINGEAL	Is cuimhin. Anois. Tá íomhá dí ag teacht chugam. Bean ghleoite is ea í. Le smideadh is béaldath dearg.
GRETA	Coinnigh ort!
AINGEAL	Tá sí gléasta go púdrach péacach. I ngúna fada.
ZOË	*(do GRETA)* Seans go bhfuil ag éirí linn, tar éis an tsaoil!
AINGEAL	Feicim ag damhsa í. Mo mháthair – tá sí ag damhsa!
ZOË	Cén saghas damhsa? Ballet, an ea?
AINGEAL	Tangó. Tá sí ag déanamh tangó.
ZOË	Léi féin?
AINGEAL	Leis an bhFear Mór.
GRETA	Anois a thuigim do chás!
ZOË	Céard eile, AINGEAL? Céard eile atá san íomhá?
AINGEAL	Tá sí ag cur a lámh thart ar a mhuineál. Seaicéad bán á chaitheamh aige. Sais ghorm. Solas ó choinnleoir ag lonrú orthu. Nuair a chasann siad is féidir diamaint a fheiceáil ar a muineálsa. Suaitheantais ar a chliabhrach. Timpeall is

timpeall leo. Tá a lámha ag sní thar a dhroim bán. Iad ag cur fola. An bán agus an gorm á ndeargadh.

GRETA   Iontach, a stór! Tá mé fíor-bhrodúil asat.

AINGEAL   An ndéanfaidh sé maith ar bith dom?

GRETA   Zoë, tá tusa anseo níos faide ná éinne eile. An ndéanfaidh an méid seo maith di?

ZOË   Tá mé ag ceapadh go ndéanfaidh. Ach ní dhéarfainn gurb í a máthair atá ag damhsa.

GRETA   Tuige?

ZOË   Ar eagla go dtabharfaí le fios gur comhoibrí í.

AINGEAL   Comhoibrí?

ZOË   Más comhluadar leapa an Fhir Mhóir í do mháthair, tabharfaí le fios go bhfuil sé ar intinn aici a mhuineál a ghearradh agus é ina chodladh. Agus go bhfuil an bheirt agaibhse ag obair as lámha a chéile.

GRETA   Níor smaoinigh mé air sin. Seans gur príosúnach í. Go bhfuil sí ag damhsa leis in aghaidh a tola.

ZOË   An príosúnach í?

AINGEAL   Tá sí i ngrá leis.

ZOË   Ach an bhfuil sí i ngéibheann?

AINGEAL   Tá. Tá sí i ngrá. Is príosúnach í. Tá sí ag dul as radharc anois. A Mhamaí! A Mhamaí, gabh i leith!

Titeann AINGEAL *ina cnap ar an úrlár.*

Celia de Fréine
Winner: Duais Foras na Gaeilge
Sponsor: Foras na Gaeilge

Richard Golden

Ireland's Disappearing Icon

*T*he thatch-roofed cottage – traditionally, one of Ireland's most enduring icons – has almost completely disapperared. A recently published report commissioned by the Department of Environment, Heritage and Local Government (DEHLG) states that thatch is being lost at an alarming rate. Although there is no comprehensive or accurate picture of the number or condition of surviving thatched buildings in Ireland it is estimated that only about 1300–1500 historic thatched homes are left in the whole of the country.

In Wexford there are roughly 500 thatched houses whilst Waterford, Galway and Clare also have strong populations. In Northern Ireland in the 1950's it was estimated that there were 40,000 thatched houses but only 150 remain today. This decline is by no means confined to the island of Ireland. In 1860 there were an estimated one million thatched houses in the UK. By 2002 this figure had fallen to around fifty thousand of which 24K were listed. Today, there is something of a revival in the use of thatch. A new thatched roof can add 10% to the value of a house – if you can find someone to do the job and can afford the price.

If you ask anybody in Ireland for an example of a typical old Irish home they are likely to point to the stone and lime-covered thatched cottage we see on postcards but they would be wrong. Contrary to popular belief, the stone-rendered cottage only became popular about 200 years ago. The true traditional Irish house was built of compacted mud but few of these old structures survive today.

> *"At one of the ends he (the cottage dweller) kept his cows, and at the other he kept his spouse" (Essyn Evans (1957))*

Mud structures have been around for thousands of years. At the time of the Famine in the 1840's it is estimated that at least for million people lived in mud houses in Ireland. In 1849, the Illustrated London News described conditions in Kilrush, Co. Clare. Most of the peasantry were said to live on the outskirts in mud homes. The less fortunate had to make do with what was described as turf sod homes otherwise known as "scalpeens". Those who were worst off lived in a "scalp", which was little more than a covered hole dug in the side of a hill.

The older house, built from local materials such as clay, stone, timber gathered from the bogs and thatch harvested from the fields, was in harmony with its surroundings. Building such humble dwellings was a community effort. There were no plans other than those in the builders' head and local styles evolved. The small windows were wider on the inside to allow more light into the house. The half-door served a similar purpose and also kept the foul out of the kitchen.

Old Irish cottages were rectangular and usually consisted of a single room between the front and rear walls. The length of the roof timbers available determined the width of the house. Since these were normally dug up from the bog the distance between the front and the rear wall was between 12 and 15 feet.

Thatch is estimated to be twice as energy efficient as a modern slate or tile roof. A thatched house is said to be warm in the winter and cool in the summer. A roof with a thickness of twelve inches at a pitch of fourty-five degrees will meet most modern insulation standards. Thatch also provides very good sound insulation. Barry O'Reilly in his book "Living Under the Thatch" (2004) points out that thatch is probably the most-used building component on the planet, followed by clay as the most common walling material.

In 1955 many Irish homeowners replaced their thatched roofs with corrugated asbestos. This change was brought about by a number of factors including cost, scarcity of materials and a shortage of thatchers. Many people were not sorry to see thatch go. Chaff falling down between the ceiling boards created dust. The sight of straw pieces blowing around the yard made the place untidy. Even fifty years ago, cost was an important reason for change – a three-roomed cottage cost about £30 to re-thatch while larger properties could cost £100 or more. For many owners, maintaining a thatched roof was simply too much trouble and expense.

The thatched house is an important part of our heritage. It is one of the most recognisable symbols of Ireland. However, for different people it conveys different powerful messages. For some, it represents a cosy past invoking an image of a thatched cottage nestling snugly into the landscape with a wisp of white smoke rising towards the sky. For others, it evokes a very different story – one of poverty, hunger and deprivation – a past they want to leave behind.

> 'We lost touch in Ireland for a few generations with our past and particularly with our architectural heritage because of a perception that it had failed us. We lost confidence in our own skills and materials and looked outside for something from someone else'
>
> *(Freda Roundtree, Chairperson of*
> *The Heritage Council, speaking on 16/11/99)*

In our eagerness to leave the past behind and embrace a better future we have lost one of our best-known icons. The image of Ireland that we promote to attract foreign tourists to our shores is now little more than a mirage. The thatched dwelling has been relegated to the postcard, porcelain replicas and cheap souvenirs in airport departure lounges. Had we known then the prosperity and economic boom which lay around the corner, perhaps, we would have not been so quick to destroy such an important part of real Ireland. That sense of connection between a house and its natural setting might not have been lost. Who knows, the whitewashed cottage may have evolved over time into the style of architecture we marvel at in countries like Spain today.

Another factor, which has contributed to the decline of the thatched roof, is the lack of suitable homegrown materials. As long ago as 1955, The Sunday Independent reported that the mechanism of farming was making life more difficult for the dying trade of the thatcher. Straw produced by the use of machinery was unsuitable for thatching which requires the use of longer lengths of straw, which the older varieties produced. The shortage of suitable thatching materials is partly due to pollution. Nitrates entering rivers and lakes cause water reeds to grow longer and faster in resulting in the reeds becoming more brittle and easily snapped. Consequently, the useful life of this material is shortened.

Water reeds are harvested for thatching from lakes and river estuaries. The reeds are cut between January and March by hand or using a mechanical reed harvester. The best reeds are grown in 15cms of non-stagnant water, which does not contain any phosphate or nitrate. One acre of reed bed can produce 250 bundles and 6–10 acres are required to thatch an average roof.

The most wonderful sights could be seen on the marshlands: kingfishers and little bearded tits, all kinds of butterflies, insects and wildflowers like ragged robin and purple loosestrife. Life for the reed cutter, out in all types of weather was hard and the sedge cut your hands. In the winter shelter from the harsh winds was a stack of reed. In the summer the reed cutter had to bear the sun beating down and the biting of insects like.

As efforts are made to close the door of the once thatched proverbial stable, we must surely hope that Ireland's historic thatched roof is not lost forever in the mists of time. It is still possible to at least slow the decline and, perhaps, bring about a revival in the use of thatch.

The DEHLG Report recommends a three-year action plan to address the issue. Proposals include placing all such buildings on a Register of Protected Structures, undertaking a systematic comprehensive survey of thatched structures, promoting local production of thatching materials, establishing a training programme for thatchers and agreeing a single specification for work on historic thatch for the whole of Ireland that regulatory and grant-giving bodies will use.

The future of thatch is in the hands of the owners of those thatched buildings that still survive and politicians who have a responsibility to preserve our rich and unique heritage. The built environment is an important part of that heritage which, if allowed to disappear through neglect or indifference, will be lost forever. In a world that is changing at an inordinate pace it is surely important to retain links and continuity with our past. (O'Reilly – 2004). Thatching has become an endangered craft and the role of the thatcher has changed too. As I said to a local thatcher working in Co. Sligo: "Susan, this is not the Ireland I knew growing up as a youth in the middle of the last century . . ."

Richard Golden
Winner of the Irish Post/Stena Line Journalism Award
Sponsors: The Irish Post/Stena Line

All that Glisters

"*H*elp, the Glitterballs fallen on Elvis Reilly," shrieked Sister Immaculata, flapping into the kitchen of St Josephs' where the St Vincent de Paul group were making sandwiches.

"Don't Panic. Leave it to me," crowed Mary as she waddled into the hall, her green kilt swaying with purpose.

"I've been curing people for over fifty years." she reassured the flock. But they weren't worried; they hadn't had this much craic since Father Dave appeared on the X factor.

"Christ. The King," she gasped, entering the hall to see Elvis splayed on the floor. His arms stretched out as a huge collar rose from the base of his neck like doves of peace. The silk lining of his cape encircled his head in a halo of virtue, as millions of splintered mirror fragments reflected its golden lining. Thick shards pierced the palms of his head and fear while a five-foot sickle of glitterball impaled his seeping body.

"He's just like Our Lord ascending into heaven," gasped Mary in awe, eyes gazing up through the smoke stained ceiling of the hall.

If anything would get her a blessing from the Pope it would be saving this man's life, she thought determinedly, rolling up her brown knitted sleeves and creped skin ready for action.

She felt a pulse of heavy breathing behind her and turned round to see that the kitchen congregation had arrived.

"We'll have him fixed in no time," she declared, ordering two paper plates from the kitchen to create some homemade kneepads. There was no point in two people being dirty, she thought, expertly placing a plate under each of her surgically stockinged knees, lowering herself heavily to the floor.

"You've got nothing to worry about now, darling. Mary's here," she soothed, flattering Elvis' well sculptured quiff in sympathy.

What a shame this had to happen in rehearsal, she sighed, as the Sacred Heart picture beheld the action from behind the bar.

"Everything's going to be fine. Rub this on your wounds, Elvis," she commanded, handing him a Miraculous Medal embossed with her namesake, Our Lady.

"This medal has been in my family for generations," she bragged. "It's renowned for its healing properties. When my brother Jimmy lost his finger in a bailing machine, we rubbed his wound with this medal and it healed over in a matter of hours. Sure, he didn't need ten fingers anyway. He can still play the spoons to this day."

Elvis had heard about this woman's sorcery, but with a huge crescent of glass growing from his chest, and his fine clothes being destroyed, what choice did he have?

"Knife," she ordered as the blood oozed from the gape in his glittery torso. Elvis wriggled on the floor in terror. He was trapped; prey in a spider's web. He knew he was about to meet his maker. As the shards of mirror pinned him to the ground, the velvet suit velcroed him to the congealed Guinness-glazed floor. There was no escape. What was she going to do? He was sure he could see the three sixes of the devil curled into her grey web of hair. She looked down, wide toothed, as he struggled for freedom.

"Jehovah, Jehovah." she yelled. "Get Jehovah for me, he's tied up outside."

Oh Shit! thought Elvis, she's got an accomplice. What am I going to do now?

His terror magnified as the St. Vincent de Paul Society realised that making sandwiches wasn't the only path to salvation.

Like shards of the glitter ball, the biddies encircled his squirming body. clones with their rosaries swinging, praying, methodically fingering the beads, counting down to his death.

"Well we've all got to do our bit to help haven't we?" whispered Nelly in the white jumper she proudly knitted in 1984. The words, "FRANKIE SAYS GO TO MASS," were boldly embroidered on her chest.

"Oh, Jehovah. Thank God you're here." sighed Mary as Nora dragged a panting Jack Russell into the hall, ears pricked, nose convulsing with pleasure at the thought of fresh meat.

Elvis fainted.

Never mind, thought Mary, I'd never have been able to make him better while he was dancing on the floor like that. You know what these stars are like; they never want to stop performing, even when they're in pain. Tommy Cooper was the very same, God Rest his Soul.

She smeared Elvis' wounds with butter.

"My Jehovah's tongue has healing properties you know," she declared. "All he has to do is lick the wounds of the sick and infirm and they're cured. Maureen Murphy had a weeping ulcer, and look at her now. She's like Michael Flatley."

The dog licked the buttered, meaty feast with gusto.

"You know he's never lost his honour either," she continued, as Nora bit her tongue, crimson with embarrassment as the thought of Jehovah sinning with the nun's prize poodle outside.

Mary dug into her musty bag, white mould fermenting in its crevices, and pulled out a Virgin Mary shaped bottle. She lovingly lifted it up to Elvis' lopsided lips.

"This will wake him up."

"AHHHHHHHHH" he screamed as he awoke with a jolt, the liquid fire scorching his tongue. He'd never sing again.

"It's a miracle!" shrieked Nelly, "He's woken from the dead! I've never seen Holy Water work like that before."

"Well the Lord works in mysterious ways," nodded Mary, her left hand concealing the poteen label taped to the Virgin Mary's toes.

The front door leapt off its hinges and swung open with a thunderous slam.

"Jesus Christ. What on earth do you think you're doing?" roared Father Dave, astonished by the spectacle he saw before him. The woman looked up stunned. All they could see was the reflection of their own virtue in the shattered glass.

"This man needs an ambulance," he screamed, kneeling down next to him, punching 999 into his Nokia 6230. That's my blessing from the Pope gone down the drain thought Mary, ruefully, lips pursed like a constipated duck. Mind you, the priest was even more handsome when he was angry, she mused, his fiery, red JFK looks glistening with passion.

He knelt down next to the injured soul like Jesus healing the lepers, bowing his head in prayer. He's so devout, thought the women.

Father Dave looked down in pity at the bleeding man, then in sorrow at the fact that his new Armani jeans had been destroyed by the blood. As he struggled to remove himself from the glazed floor, the paramedics stormed into the church hall and rushed the tortured body of Elvis to the hospital.

"I've never seen a wound so expertly cleaned," said the chief paramedic as he sped out of the hall.

"That was my Jehovah," replied Mary, swelling with pride. The women congratulated each other on a job well done, while Father Dave rushed out of the hall, lit up a fag to steady his nerves and leapt on his motorbike to follow the ambulance.

"Well, what are those poor children in Africa going to do now that we have no Elvis to sing at our Benefit Dance tonight?" cried Mary. She scaffolded her ample mammeries with her crossed arms.

"We'll never raise any money now."

"Well, we could call Patelvis," whispered Nelly.

"Who on earth is Pat-Elvis?"

"He works at the Indian restaurant down the road you know, Balti Towers,"

"We can't have him. He's Muslin or Hen-do or one of those heathen religions!" cried Nora.

"Well he must have Irish roots with a first name like Pat. There's surely some Catholic in him somewhere. Anyway, what choice do we have? It's a Catch 28 situation," sighed Mary, throwing her arms in the air with dismay.

"Don't you mean Catch 22?" asked Nelly pensively.

"Oh no. It's way worse than that. If we don't phone him hundreds of African Children will starve, and if we do we'll have to let a heathen into our church hall. Well this is an emergency!" yelled Mary, grabbing the Yellow Pages from behind the bar, licking her thumb and furiously searching for the number of Balti Towers. Maybe this would get her a blessing from the Pope. She stabbed the number into the telephone and asked to speak to Patelvis.

"He'll surely agree to play for us tonight," she told her captive audience, "they have starving children in India too you know."

That night Patelvis was greeted with uproarious applause from the pensioners of St Joseph's as he glistened to the tune of "Glory Glory Alleluia."

"He's one of our own," they agreed.

I knew it would work," cheered Mary, pointing to the yellow warning lights they'd borrowed from the edge of a manhole on Holloway Road.

"It's just like Las Vegas."

As the golden beacons flashed in time with Patelvis' gyrating hips. Elvis Reilly staggered out of the hospital and disappeared down an unmarked manhole.

"Sure, who needs a glitterball anyway?"

Carmel Walsh
Winner of the Irish Post/Stena Line – Short Story Award
Sponsors: The Irish Post/Stena Line

Blonde Ambition

At thirteen years of age a young boy falls in love very easily. Danny of course fell for his neighbour, Tina. It was a long hot summer, one of the hottest on record for the west of Ireland, a summer that was to change Danny's life in an extraordinary way.

Before Tina moved into the house next door, Danny was lonely. It was the early eighties in Ireland, a time when the best chance of getting work was to jump on a ferry to England and join the boom on London's building sites. Danny's father did just that. Danny was one of five children and his father Tim came from hard working stock. He eventually made the hard decision to take that ferry. As the summer went on the money stopped coming from England and Danny got the feeling that somehow his Dad just wasn't going to come back. Danny began to feel very insecure, his mother began treating him harshly. He wasn't to know that it pained her to be around Danny, a boy so like his father in looks and personality. His mother would cry a lot and then lose her temper. This made Danny want to play outside more and more.

Danny nearly dropped when he saw Tina. He was immediately smitten. His mother said new neighbours had moved in and he and his little brother Jimmy went round to have a look. She was an eyeful! Six foot tall, blonde hair, bright blue eyes, and lips that Danny would kiss over and over again in his dreams. He walked around in an endless trance of innocent infatuation. She was about 23 at the time and lived with her boyfriend, their five year old kid Sam, and a beautiful golden retriever called Max. Tina's boyfriend didn't spend much time at home. He worked in Galway and had to travel eighty miles to get to work. Tina was often left on her own for days on end.

This gave Danny the opportunity to drop in on Tina all the time to help her out. He was always in the house asking Tina if she needed coal or anything from the shop. He was constantly by her side and when sometimes his mother would call Danny home, like iron from a magnet, Danny would tear his innocent 4 foot 5 skinny frame away from Tina's side. "Go on Danny", Tina would say. "Your Mum is looking for you". Tina's soft English accent would run riot through Danny's heart. She always spoke softly to Danny, for she relied on him like a younger brother.

Weeks went by and Tina's boyfriend spent more and more time away from home. Eventually he didn't seem to be around at all. Only now looking back on it Danny saw that she fell on tough times with her boyfriend.

Danny's dream was soon to be shattered. Tina never told him she was leaving for good. It simply happened. One day she called Danny and asked him would he do her a big favour. She said that she had to go home to England for a little while and that she had no one to take care of Max. "I've asked around", she said "and nobody will take Max because he is too big".

"I'll take him", Danny eagerly replied, "I'll take him and I'll mind him for you until you come back."

"No Danny, your mother wouldn't let you". Tina sat beside him on the couch and stroked his sun burnt face.

"You're a good boy Danny, like a brother to me", Danny was smitten.

"Danny, I need you to drown Max for me". Without a single thought Danny jumped up and said "OK Tina".

All summer long Danny had not only been part of this new family but Max had adopted him. It was plain to see that this two and a half year old semi – giant absolutely adored Danny with every fun-loving shake of his wavy body. Danny had always been such a good boy. He loved animals, he was always so caring with them, his emotions now ran deeper because all he could feel was the loss of his father. Yet when Tina casually asked "Danny love, will you take Max down to the river for me and drown him", he was so starry eyed that without question he replied "OK, Tina".

Danny took Max's lead and Max jumped with excitement expecting his walk, as Danny used to take Max for walks regularly. Danny arrived at the local pond and stopped beside the man-made concrete bank. It was such a beautiful spot, the water was as clear as drinking water and about 10 foot deep. Danny remembers going in to the wood and getting a rock the size of a concrete block. He tied it to the dog's rope. He knelt down and looked the dog in the eyes. Max stared back at Danny as Danny stroked him behind the ears. Max had a sullen expression on his face as if in knowing his fate. Danny felt nothing as he was about to do this cruel deed. He just had a sense that he had a job to do and that he was a good boy that always done as he was told.

Danny again patted Max on the head as he lifted the rock. With his knee he pushed Max into the water and the heavy stone pulled Max to the bottom. Because of the hot summer the water wasn't as deep as Danny thought it would be. Max was only about two feet from the surface and he was fighting for his life. Danny gazed at Max with a deep intense stare. Danny felt nothing. He felt no pleasure, no pain, no emotion. Nothing. In his head he knew what he had to do. He was asked to do something and he did. Max lost his fight to the water and Danny walked away.

Since that day Danny has learned to do things in a way that if something has to be done, then that is the way to do it. Take no pleasure, feel no pain, take no pride. Empty the mind of all emotion. "Just get the job done".

To this day what strikes Danny as unusual was the fact that he had never hurt anything before that time. He loved animals and at the innocent age of thirteen fell in love with this nice woman who lived next door to him, this woman who out of the blue asked him to kill her dog. All this woman ever saw was the love of a teen which was loyal and pure.

When Danny got home Tina was gone. She had made the choice to return to England with Sam for good. She never said goodbye. Danny never met this woman again. Years later Danny would wonder how she knew that he had this quality, whatever quality that enabled him to commit such an act. A quality which lead Danny to where he dwells today. He never asks for any job, it's always offered.

Danny was drinking on his own in a pub one night, years later. It was one of those nights when the rain was falling heavily outside. As he sat with his elbows on the countertop and his hands and fingers entwined around the glass, he was a man about to make a decision whether to have another pint or go home.

Suddenly Danny felt a hand resting on his shoulder. He turned his head and there was this blonde haired woman behind him. She was well dressed and quite beautiful. She spoke softly into his ear and they engaged in deep conversation. She asked him to do something for her which would merit a price. He never met this woman before and after he did what she paid him to do, he never met her again.

Afterwards an empty feeling of nothingness came over him again, just like that feeling when he gazed into that dog's eyes.

Danny again asks himself today how this stranger who had never seen him before knew to walk across a bar and request his services. She was a stranger to him then and remains a stranger to him today as so many others have remained strangers to Danny for a long period of time.

Shadows in the night never pass as Danny dwells in his prison cell.

Michael Scanlon
Winner: Short Story, Writing in Prisons – Ireland and Overseas
Sponsors: Department of Justice/Prisons Education Services

The Period

I watch as you squat
on a landscape
a chocolate box
Picturesque. A Monet.
Masterpiece he would never paint.
You are surrounded by poppies in the morning summer sun.

Rivulets jewelled rubies
and diamonds, faceted by light
make their way down your thighs.
Colours of magenta, vermillion and crimson
rivulets of your blood, turn into tributaries
long before they hit the ground.

John Mold

The great war on this very field
thousands of young men sacrificed their blood
willingly and copiously,
so you could, in a couple of generations
have a life of freedom.

Arnold Clarke
Winner: Poetry, Writing in Prisons – Overseas
Sponsors: The Irish Commission for Prisons Overseas

Tax return for Genghis Khan. . . Returned!

. . . "my records for that year are rather rough"
is simply not good enough, not good enough
at all; and as for "I was busy in foreign lands
taking new territories with my own bloody hands" . . .
your Accountant should have made it perfectly clear
that Tax Amendment One-O-One (recently passed here)
was retrospective for two-point-five hundred years.
It means – sine qua non – that you were there

and – tax-wise – simultaneously here as soon
as you and your "Warriors Of The Crescent Moon"
(successfully) invaded Chinese soil.
Had you – by indigenous opponents – been foiled
all Dirt Tax extracted for gains during such "Incursive Time"
would have been reimbursed (on completing Form Nine-O-Nine)

– after your locust armies had Officially Retreated
from China as – both parties agreeing – "The Defeated".

Regarding "Additional Permanent Expenses" . . .
we are – as you rightly note – indeed "ring-fencing"
"(Singular And) Multiple Allowances For Plural Wives"
However – at point of claim – they must all still be alive!
Mistresses like "Murder-In-Laws" do not qualify
however much "they [may] bleed a mere man dry".
Similarly "Personal Professional Allowances", My Lord,
covers one to five, not purchasing five thousand swords.

Further: you should understand that vaguely noting "sundry booty"
does not qualify as a "Full And Exhaustive Inventory
Of Other Pillaged Martial Campaign Gains", nor explain
"somehow making a loss" selling nine hundred prisoners in chains.
Accordingly, Sire, you still inhabit the Highest Tax Rate
and must promptly pay in full as detailed on the following slate.
Late Restitution Will Not Be Tolerated and Will Incur
an immediate confiscation of eight million fur

pelts and lengthy Community Service among the poor
and the down-town lepers (tending suppurating sores).
(This is The Middle Ages not The Dark Ages
– for all that a certain tax evader annually rages!)
Investigations Into Multiple Tax Benefit Claims
are currently exposing many to prison and shame . . .
Since Eleven-Eighty-Four one Temujin has also claimed
in your script using your address. Please can you explain?

John Mold
Winner: Poetry, Writing in Prisons – Ireland & Overseas
Sponsors: Department of Justice/Prisons Education Service

Escape

A hush descended on the courtroom as the judge shuffled the paperwork spread before him The barristers were busy organising the files for their next case. The reporters were scribbling away on their notepads and the prosecuting detectives were smirking in my direction.

As any criminal will attest, these agonising moments every judge takes before passing sentence can be endless. It's when the knees shake a little and the palms of your hands become sweaty knowing your fate lies with this little bespectacled man in a funny looking wig. I was trying to look as placid and remorseful as I could when he finally looked up from all that damning data, removed his spectacles, and looked disdainfully . . . at me.

> "These offences are of a serious nature, Your criminal record is substantial to say the least, Mr Smith, so I have no alternative but to impose a custodial sentence."

Every judge sinks into another endless minute of silence once he has reached that decision, I don't know why, but I think they rather enjoy it. They tell you that you're going to jail, let it sink in for a minute or two, and then make a little speech.

> "I have taken into account the difficulty of your circumstances at the time of these events, and also the fact that you have pleaded guilty to the offences."

Another endless pause, "I sentence you to three years imprisonment."

I steal a quick glance to my left and see Detective John Nicholson looking triumphantly at his giant, ginger-haired partner, John McHale, and I curse them both under my breath.

I am handcuffed and sitting in the back seat of a police car on the way down the Dublin Road to Mountjoy Prison. John McHale is on my left and John Nicholson on my right. Both of them are in good form as they laugh and joke about the menu on offer in Mountjoy.

"You'll get used to the cockroaches in no time, Glen," McHale chuckles. He tells me the Christmas dinner is not too bad, as he lights his cigarette.

"I'll be having my dinner at home, John," I replied.

This statement had them laughing harder. But I wasn't joking; I had other plans. I'd already had a small taste of Mountjoy Prison, an ancient pile of Victorian grey brick, full of dead-eyed heroin addicts, mice infested cells, and the constant smell of urine wherever you went.

We arrived at the jail around 5 o'clock and I watched the big green doors opening and a screw wave the car through. The gate closed slowly and, inch by inch, the daylight faded, taking my freedom with it.

"Welcome to the 'Joy'!" My handcuffs were removed and, after handing over the warrants to the prison officer, John One and John Two gave me a parting smile and wished me well before I was led me away to be processed.

In the prison Reception area every new arrival is obliged to give all his personal details. What's your full name? Next of kin? Have you ever been here before? Any tattoos? Any Scars? Any illness, medication requirements or allergies? "Go take a shower".

Sentenced prisoners are issued with the prison uniform of grey trousers (that <u>never</u> fit!), a green shirt, a grey V-neck jumper and white trainers. Worst of all is the underwear: a white vest and a pair of white cotton Y-fronts your granddad wouldn't wear. I remember looking in the mirror and laughing at the thought of the missus seeing me now!

All sentenced prisoners to Mountjoy are sent to B-Wing. The walls are a sickly yellow colour and the cell doors are dark green. Very little daylight manages to squeeze in through the filth of the windows and the stink of urine is everywhere.

Scores of lifeless smack-heads shuffle up and down the wing in prison-issue duffle coats, looking bored and lost. I stop at the gate and notice the grime on the walls. I'm in a nightmare. I'm shown my cell and the door is slammed and locked behind me, leaving me to take in my new surroundings. The paint on the walls is flaking off and the names of past residents are written everywhere. I can hear the cars and buses outside and I jump up on the bed and look through the old, rusted bars at the North Circular Road. Freedom! So near, yet so far. I can see people walking; men and women hand in hand. I think about the girl I love, hundreds of miles away in Derry. I realise that it might as well be a million miles now. I make my bed up and lie down to rest. I fall into an exhausted sleep.

The night I escaped was two weeks later. A fortnight of such surroundings, not having anyone to talk to, and heartbreaking phone-calls to my girlfriend had the same thought going through my head constantly – I had to get out of this place.

We were locked up for the night about eight o'clock and I started making my preparations immediately. I used the sheet on my bed to make my 'rope'. I hid this under my pillow and waited for the screw to do his hourly check. Every hour you could hear the click, click of the officer's shoes as he went from cell to cell, peeping through the spy-holes on the cell doors. I pretended to be reading a book when I heard him at my door. When he moved on to the next cell I got up and ripped a page from the book, covered it with toothpaste and stuck it on the door where the peephole was. Now I had to wait.

I tied my sheet tightly around the bars on my window, making sure to leave enough room for my noose at the end. I put the noose around my neck and let the sheet take all my weight, testing it for strength. A good job! I judged that almost an hour had passed so I stood close to the cell door and listened for the clicking shoes. Then I heard it. He was coming. I moved quickly to the window and slipped the noose around my neck. The footsteps grew closer and closer until I heard my spy-hole being opened. There was a moment's silence, "Glen Smith? Take that off right now!"

I kept silent. My heart was pounding and my breath shallow. The screw repeated the order. I ignored it and, as I anticipated, he sped off to inform his senior officer. I knew they'd both be back with the keys.

While I was waiting for them to come I tightened the noose a little around my throat and held my breath to create the purple face of a hanging man. I let some saliva drool from the corners of my mouth and just as I heard the keys being placed in the lock I tightened the noose more and let my body flop, limp and lifeless. There was a, "Jaysus Christ!" and the rushing of bodies as my head started to spin and I felt my legs being lifted off the ground.

"Get an ambulance!" I heard one of them stutter, as I was laid out in the recovery position on the cold, concrete floor. I added a few gurgling noises in my throat, one or two convulsions and twitching legs for good effect. "He's fairly serious, Mickey!"

Music to my ears!

The slaps on my face stung and the nips on my inner thighs were sore but once you've gone this far you go into automatic. I was going all the way now.

I was taken on a stretcher to the Mater Hospital, directly across the street from Mountjoy prison. I decided it would be wise to start gaining consciousness at this point in order to take in my surroundings. I was looking for windows and exit doors as I was taken to the X-ray department. An Indian doctor hurried into the room and examined my neck.

"We need to X-ray your neck to make sure nothing is damaged," he said. The three screws sent to guard me stood silent but watchful. Their eyes told me that they weren't entirely convinced.

When I was X-rayed I was taken to a small room where I was handcuffed to the silver bars on the hospital bed. A nurse took my pulse and left the room. The screws just watched me quietly. Outside I looked calm and distant but inside my mind was racing and the adrenaline was surging through every muscle in my body.

The Indian doctor entered the room and asked me if I had taken any drugs that night as my pulse was very slow. Earlier I'd taken some tablets – forty milligrams of Valium – and I'd smoked a joint too. "No, I don't take drugs," I mumbled.

"We are going to keep you for three hours' observation," said the doctor. "Brilliant," I said, in my head of course.

The observation room was small, no bigger that the cell in the prison. The screws, realising they'd be here for a while, decided to take turns going for cups of tea. Screw one left the room for his break and the other two were left to keep an eye on the prisoner. One of them sat at the foot of my bed reading a newspaper. The other sat at a small table and busied himself with a crossword puzzle.

I watched each of them closely for a few minutes and neither seemed too concerned with the thought that I might be planning to bolt. I looked at the bars on the bed to which I was cuffed. They ran the full length of the bed. I slipped my free hand under the blanket and began probing and testing the bars. I nearly fell out the bed when, with very little effort, I found that the bars came away from each other at the middle.

Now my heart was pumping and the energy in my body was so powerful I thought I would explode. I used my foot to push at the bars at the bottom of the bed while my hand pulled at the top end. I could feel them coming apart. I watched the screws closely while doing this. Neither of them moved. The bars came away from each other just far enough for me to slip the cuffs gently off. I was free.

It's hard to explain all the different feelings going through my mind and body in those following minutes. The room was small and I was in an awkward position on the bed. If I didn't do this in one fluid movement the screws would be upon me and there would be a struggle. I didn't want any violence if possible.

It took me a while to build up the courage to make a break for it. I counted in my head, one, two, three! Adrenaline took over at this point and no matter how many times I try and remember those next thirty seconds, it's always a blur. I remember a newspaper being thrown in the air. I remember hearing cursing and panic, and the flinging of chairs as I flew off the bed and out the door.

But my favourite memory of it all was the automatic doors at the entrance to the Casualty Department. On my arrival I'd noticed how slowly these doors opened and I'd feared by the time they opened now that the two screws would be jumping all over me. As I sprinted for the doors an elderly couple were coming into the hospital. The doors opened perfectly to meet my stride and I hurdled the railings, landed running and never once looked back.

The shouting faded with every yard I ran until I disappeared into a maze of streets and back lanes. I ran up one of these lanes and hopped over a wall into the back garden of a house. I remember the houses were all red-brick, terraced houses and the lanes and streets made me think of Coronation Street for some reason. I hid out in a small garden shed and fell asleep under a big cardboard box.

When I woke up I was shivering. When I first arrived at the hospital the nurses had used scissors to cut my shirt and pullover off, so I was naked from the waist up. I looked out the small window of the shed. It was getting bright. I guessed it must have been around six in the morning.

The garden I was in was long and quite narrow. A clothesline ran the length of the lawn and on it were shirts, T-shirts and towels. I had to smile. I came out of the shed cautiously. I watched the windows as I reached up and pulled a shirt from the line. I then pulled down a tea-towel. I used this to wrap around the handcuffs still attached to my right arm. It would have to do for now.

I jumped over the wall and started running. I didn't know where I was but ran from alley to alley, listening for the sound of car engines before darting to the next one.

Eventually I ended up on some train tracks and I just kept running until I felt I had covered enough miles. Then I came to a taxi office.

I took a taxi to a place called Tallaght where I had a friend. I had to knock the whole family up. I had spun the taxi-driver a yarn about being at a party and cutting my arm on a broken bottle to explain the towel wrapped around my arm. My pal in Tallaght was confused at first but when I explained what had happened we had a good laugh. He used a hacksaw to remove the handcuffs. He kept them as a trophy and still has them today.

I did spend Christmas at home, and made sure to send John One and John Two a Christmas card! Inside I wrote: "I told you I'd be home for Xmas!"

The two Johns and I were to meet again – but that's another story!

Glen Smith
Winner: Autobiography, Writing in Prisons
Sponsors: Department of Justice/Prisons Education Service

Sean Tadhg

Sona ag caitheamh a phiopaí,
Bhí a am anois aibí.

Sheol an cogar ar aghaidh,
Tá tú uaim, a Thadhg.

Tháinig siad ó bhfad agus gar,
cuid ar rothar cuid i gcarr.

Tionól mór anall,
Cléir ag siúl go mall.

Deoch agus caint eatorra,
Cuimhní caoin ar a hata.

Paddy Deery
Winner: Irish Section, Writing in Prisons
Sponsors: Depertmant of Justice/Prisons Education Service

The Fir Tree and the Ivy

Scene 5   *December 1933. The area immediately in front of Heidegger's cabin at Todtnauberg in the Black Forest. It has been snowing. There is a camp fire with log benches around it, together with, at one end, a rustic, dark-wood "carver" chair.* HEIDEGGER *himself is chopping wood and making the logs into a pile, now and again putting one on the fire to keep it going. He is dressed in a knickerbocker version of a Nazi Party uniform, a swastika symbol in his button-hole. Gradually* FOUR YOUTHS, *blond, athletic and in Nazi Student Youth uniform, emerge from the cabin, giving Heidegger a Nazi "Heil Hitler" salute, to which he briefly responds in kind, and then saying "Guten Morgen" to him and to each other. They stand watching Heidegger.*

Heidegger *(After a few moments, ceasing his wood-chopping, putting the axe aside and looking at his pocket watch.)* You lazy lumps should've been up an hour ago and running in the forest, or chopping wood, Good for the soul.

  (Ruminatively.) Only up here, in the forest, in my mountain retreat, do I really feel myself alive. In Freiburg I feel flabby, and fear I'll become like my effeminate colleagues. But up here, in the snow, and the frosty air, with no distractions, my mind is hard, like steel. Here one is away from the toys of civilization, One is plunged into the pure and simple life. *(Pause.)* It's here that I wrote *Being and Time*. And it's here I hope to write so much more.

  (After another pause, in professorial mode.)

  Well, set yourselves down.

  (The four students seat themselves on the benches around the fire facing Heidegger who sits on his "carver" chair.)

I should thank you for accepting my invitation to this winter camp. I hope to invite you again in the summer, to continue our work together. But this morning we must make a beginning, before we become too cold and are driven indoors. A *new* beginning.

(*Pause.*) I invited you here, something I wouldn't normally do, for a special reason. I invited you here because you're the student leaders at the university. You are my stormtroopers. I expect much of you and much support from you. I expect each one of us to move forward together to actualize his role in the total transformation, the *Gleichschaltung*, of our German universities, and the will-to-knowledge of our German people. For this is our destiny, made possible at last by the passion and power of our Fuhrer. The truth is not for everyone, but only for the strong. His strength, his unflinching strength, has brought into being for each one of us the will to answer for oneself, to confront and declare our Being, to nurture it to its full awakening, throughout the whole nation. We must not fail him in the battles ahead.

(*Pausing to get his thoughts straight.*)

But we must move forward together in the right spirit.

What is this spirit?

It is the spirit of *authenticity*. In so far as any human acknowledges authentically his Being-in-the-world, his *Dasein*, then he or she is truly resolute and in a state of anticipation, but it is an anxious anticipation of the very possibilities at the core of his existence. Our human existence alone lays this burden on us, because we alone are not beings merely present-at-hand or ready-to-hand. We are Beings-in-the-world. We know this in our depths, even if we still refuse to acknowledge it. Even if we fall at times, too busy listening to the world's chatter. We *alone* know that we are not mere facts or artifacts in the universe. We *alone* know our temporality, that each of us is potentiality-for-Being, yet we are all burdened with the urgency and angst of our Being-towards-death which is the end of all possibilities. We *alone* know that to be *resolute* is to be prepared to exact anxiety of ourselves and take care for the future in the face of this terrible truth, this coruscating disclosure.

Conscience is what calls us back to acknowledging, authentically, our existential predicament. Knowing of our continual everyday falling back into the *they*-world, our failure to confront the absurdity and nothingness of our own lonely self-predicament is knowledge of our original sin, the source of our existential guilt. Conscience is the prophylactic against out tranquillizing self-concealment, the alarm bell warning of self-delusion, the minatory voice forbidding us draw back from laying bare the primordial ontology of our Being-in-the-world, rebuffing any denial that we are essentially Beings-in-time, annihilating any refusal to acknowledge that everything, absolutely everything, is up to us, to *each of us* as individuals.

In our rare moments of angst or dread, or confronted by some defining decision, we catch a searing glimpse of the lonely majesty of our very Being-in-the-world, and its peremptory summons. History imagined only historically does not tell us what is essential about human existence. Length of duration gives us no insight into Being. It is the radical moment, the now of rapture or rupture. It is the momentary sky-searing illumination of the lightning that plunges us into Being. This lightning flash is summoning us now. Answering this summons is not optional, not a matter of discretion. It is *commanded* of us, *demanded* of us. Because we can, and know we can, we must answer the call to self-disclosure. We must answer the call to live the contradiction of potentiality facing the abyss of nothingness.

Today, this hour, this minute, we are facing such a summons and a decision as never before. Our moment, the defining moment for each of us, has come. So there can be no retreat, no position of acceptable ignorance, no escape, no excuse, no apologia, no derogation of our decision to others, no hiding place.

(Standing suddenly to attention and extending his arm in the Deutscher Gruss salute.)

Heil Hitler!

(They stand up immediately, obediently, and return his salute. He then "stands easy", looks down at the ground then around at the rural view, and finally at the students.)

We shall resume our ruminations again after lunch, at exactly 2 p.m. Between now and lunch, I shall take you on a walk in the Black Forest, so that, like the fir trees, we can breathe the pure clear air and clear our spirits of chatter.

But first, to let us sing!

(Heidegger and the student leaders line up facing the audience and launch into the Horst Wessel song, in German:

Die Fahne hoch die Reihen fest geschlossen
S.A. marschiert mit ruhig festem Schritt,
Kam 'raden die Rotfront . . . etc.

As the curtain comes down on this first Act, the five voices are overtaken by the sound of a massed choir, with military band accompaniment, singing the same song.)

William Lyons
Winner: The Eamon Keane Full Length Play Award
Sponsors: Spectra Photo Group